Amazing Animal
Shape-Shifters

by Leon Gray

CAPSTONE PRESS
a capstone imprint

Fact Finders are published by Capstone Press,
1710 Roe Crest Drive, North Mankato, Minnesota 56003
www.capstonepub.com

Published in 2016 by Capstone Publishers, Ltd.
Copyright © 2016 Brown Bear Books Ltd.

Library of Congress Cataloging-in-Publication Data
Cataloging-in-publication information is on file with the Library of Congress

ISBN: 978-1-4914-6983-5 (hardcover)
ISBN: 978-1-4914-6993-4 (paperback)
ISBN: 978-1-4914-7003-9 (eBook PDF)

For Brown Bear Books Ltd:
Text: Leon Gray
Editor: Tim Harris
Picture Researcher: Clare Newman
Designer: Karen Perry
Design Manager: Keith Davis
Production Director: Alastair Gourlay
Editorial Director: Lindsey Lowe
Children's Publisher: Anne O'Daly

Photo Credits
Front cover: Cathy Keifer/Shutterstock
1, Cathy Keifer/Shutterstock; 4, Chris T Pehlivan/ Shutterstock; 5tr, Tylinek/Shutterstock; 5bl, Dmitry Rukhlenko/iStock/
Thinkstock; 5bc, Cuson/Shutterstock; 6brs, Paul Reeves Photography /Shutterstock; 6-7background, B. and E. Dudzinscy /
Shutterstock; 6-7, IrinaK/Shutterstock; 7br, Dirk Ercken/Shutterstock; 8, Vitalii Hulai /Shutterstock; 8-9t, manzrussali /Shutterstock;
9b, Anatoliy Lukich/Shutterstock; 11t, Cuson/Shutterstock; 11b, Dirk Ercken /Shutterstock; 12br, Raul Rouzon/National
Geographic Image Collection/Alamy; 12-13, Ken Griffitha/NHPA/Photoshot; 13t, Masahiro Suzuki /Shutterstock; 14, Stubblefield
Photography/Shutterstock; 15t, nicolas.voisin44/Shutterstock; 15b, aquapix/Shutterstock; 16, Alain Compost/Biosphoto/FLPA;
17t, A J Wilhelm/National Geographic Image Collection/Alamy; 17b, David Tipling/Alamy; 18, Andrew Astbury /Shutterstock;
18-19, dibrova /Shutterstock; 19t, Cathy Keifer/Shutterstock; 20, Cathy Keifer/Shutterstock; 21t, Dmitry Rukhlenko/iStock/
Thinkstock; 21b, Cathy Keifer/Shutterstock; 22, J L Klein & M L Hubert/FLPA; 23t, outdoorsman /Shutterstock; 23b, ©Still FX/
Shutterstock; 24, Luke Suen/Shutterstock; 24-25, LFRabanedo/Shutterstock; 25t, Ellen Stenard/iStock/Thinkstock; 26, Nagel
Photography/Shutterstock; 27t, Przemek Tokar/Shutterstock; 27b, Aditya Singh/Getty Images; 28, Michael Stubblefield/Alamy;
29t, Stuart F. Westmorland/Danita Delimont/Alamy; 29b, Ethan Daniels/Alamy.
t=top, c=center, b=bottom, l=left, r=right

All Artworks © Brown Bear Books Ltd
Brown Bear Books has made every attempt to contact the copyright holder.
If you have any information please contact licensing@brownbearbooks.co.uk

Printed in China

Table of Contents

Introduction

The world is full of creatures that change their shape or color. Some animals change shape as they grow older. Others change their shape or color to blend in with their surroundings.

When a caterpillar changes shape and turns into a butterfly, this change is called metamorphosis. Other animals make similar changes as they get older. Legless tadpoles become frogs with four legs. Young dragonflies live in water and are wingless. They change into flying insects.

Squid, octopuses, and cuttlefish squeeze their bodies into different shapes. They do this to look like pieces of coral or other animals when they are hiding from **predators**.

Other animals change color. Some male birds lose their feathers in spring. They grow new, brighter feathers to attract female birds. This change usually takes a few weeks. Chameleons can change color in just a few minutes.

Animals perform the most amazing changes of shape or color as they grow and to stay safe.

Winter colors

Some creatures change color with the seasons. Hares, foxes, and stoats are brown or gray in the spring or summer. Their fur turns white in winter when snow lies on the ground. They change color so that they can blend with their surroundings.

Soldiers who train in snowy places wear white clothing and face masks. The soldiers are camouflaged, just like the animals.

COPYCAT

Scientists at the Massachusetts Institute of Technology designed screens wi inks that v similar wa chromato a chamele

WOW

South American poison dart frogs release **toxic** chemicals onto their skin. The chemical acts as a defense against predators. Poison dart frogs are usually brightly colored. Their bright colors warn other animals not to eat them.

Guide for readers

Throughout this book, special feature boxes accompany the main text, captioned photographs, and illustrations. COPYCAT boxes highlight some of the ways in which people have been inspired by the animal world. WOW boxes provide incredible facts and figures about different animals.

M tamorphosis

Dogs, cats, and horses look like big versions of puppies, kittens, and foals. However, some animals go through amazing changes to become adults. These changes are called metamorphosis.

Caterpillars and butterflies

A caterpillar hatches from an egg. It spends all its time eating leaves. As it grows, the caterpillar sheds its skin five or six times. When the caterpillar is ready to become a butterfly, a hard shell, or pupa, forms around its body. Inside the pupa, the body of the caterpillar breaks down and new butterfly body parts form. The pupa then splits open, and the adult butterfly emerges. The butterfly looks nothing like the pupa or the caterpillar.

Amphibians, such as frogs and salamanders, also go through metamorphosis. So do other animals, such as jellyfish. A jellyfish starts life as a small, swimming **larva**. The larva settles on a rock, and its shape changes. It becomes a **polyp**, which has **tentacles** and catches passing prey. Eventually, parts of the polyp break away and float off into the water. Each part grows into an adult jellyfish.

An adult dragonfly has four wings. Younger dragonflies do not have wings and cannot fly.

DRAGONFLIES CASE STUDY: PAGE 10

This caterpillar will change first into a pupa and then transform into a beautiful butterfly.

This poison dart frog has grown from a tadpole. Unlike tadpoles, adult frogs can live outside water.

FROGS CASE STUDY: PAGE 8

FROGS CASE STUDY: PAGE 8

7

Dragonflies

Adult dragonflies are flying insects with two pairs of wings and large eyes. These colorful creatures survive for only a few weeks after becoming adults. Before they become adults, dragonflies live underwater.

Dragonfly larvae look nothing like adults. They live and hunt in water.

Living in water

After mating, a female dragonfly lays hundreds of eggs in a stream or lake about a week later. A larva hatches from each egg. The young dragonfly larvae are called nymphs. They spend the next couple of years in water. Nymphs breathe using **gills**. They eat as much as they can during this stage in their **life cycle**. The youngest nymphs eat the larvae of other insects. When they get older and bigger the nymphs eat bigger **prey**. Sometimes they even eat small fish.

A dragonfly nymph grows in stages. At each stage, the nymph sheds its hard outer covering, or exoskeleton. A new one is underneath. The new exoskeleton is **flexible** for a while. This means the nymph can continue to grow. Each time the nymph sheds its exoskeleton, it grows a little bigger.

Eventually the nymph climbs out of the water. It attaches itself to a plant and puffs up its body with air. The old exoskeleton cracks open, and an adult dragonfly squeezes out of it. The dragonfly spreads its wings to dry them. Then it flies away to hunt mosquitoes and other small insects. It will also look for a mate so it can complete its life cycle.

COPYCAT

Dragonflies can fly forward at up to 35 miles (56 km) per hour. They can also fly backward, though much more slowly. Just like dragonflies, helicopters can also fly forward and backward.

Frogs

Frogs belong to a group of animals called amphibians. Frogs spend several weeks of their lives as tadpoles in ponds or rivers. Slowly, the tadpoles change shape and become adult frogs.

A life in water

There are more than 6,400 different kinds of frogs. They live all over the world. Some live in lakes, rivers, and rain forests. Other frogs live in tiny backyard ponds. Wherever they live, all frogs need water in which to lay their eggs. Some frogs live in water most of their lives. Others live in dry places much of the year and only visit water when it is time for them to breed.

Tadpoles with long tails emerge from frogspawn. Tadpoles grow four legs and lose their tail as they first become young frogs, then adult frogs.

Life cycle

Like other amphibians, a frog begins life as an egg. A female frog lays thousands of eggs. These float on the surface of the water in clumps called frogspawn. Most of the eggs are eaten by fish, insect larvae, ducks, and herons. Only a few survive and hatch into tadpoles.

A tadpole has a long tail but no legs. Like a fish, it has gills to breathe in water. For the first few weeks of its life, a tadpole swims in water. It feeds on **algae** and tries to avoid predators. The tadpole begins to change shape as it grows older. It grows four tiny legs, and lungs form inside its body. At this stage it is called a young frog, or froglet.

The young frog grows bigger. Its mouth becomes wider, its tail gets shorter, and its legs grow longer. When its lungs are fully grown, the young frog can begin to breathe air. It is now an adult frog and can leave the water for the first time.

WOW

South American poison dart frogs release **toxic** chemicals onto their skin. The chemical acts as a defense against predators. Poison dart frogs are usually brightly colored. Their bright colors warn other animals not to eat them.

This adult red-eyed tree frog has feet that are good at clinging to branches.

Changing Shape

Some animals have amazing shape-shifting powers when they are fully grown. They can change their shape when they are scared or angry, when they are hiding, or when they are attracting mates.

Sizes and shapes

Some lizards spread a frill of skin around their neck when they are threatened. This makes them look more frightening and may scare off a predator.

Animals with soft bodies are the best shape-shifters. They can change the shape of their body more easily than an animal with a bony skeleton. Octopuses escape from predators by squeezing into tiny holes in rocks on the ocean floor.

Male birds often change their shape to attract a mate. Peacocks fan out their colorful tail feathers. Male birds of paradise stretch their wings and spread their tail. Some birds of paradise can change shape until they no longer look like a bird.

A bird of paradise changes its shape when it spreads its wings.

BIRDS OF PARADISE CASE STUDY: PAGE 16

Cuttlefish are shape-shifting creatures of ocean waters.

**CUTTLEFISH CASE STUDY:
PAGE 14**

A frill-necked lizard warns off predators by spreading the frill around its neck and opening its mouth wide.

Cuttlefish

The cuttlefish is a master of disguise. This ocean creature changes its shape to blend in with its surroundings. The cuttlefish does this to trick its prey and to escape from predators.

This cuttlefish has pulled its arms close. It looks like part of the seafloor.

Arms and tentacles

Cuttlefish are **mollusks**, not fish. They have large eyes, eight arms, and two tentacles covered with suction cups. Most cuttlefish live in shallow water near coral reefs and rocks. They eat crabs and fish, which they grab with their suction cups. It is easy for prey to spot a swimming cuttlefish and escape from it. A hungry cuttlefish has a way around this problem. It disguises itself so that its prey cannot see it. The cuttlefish swims to the seafloor and draws its arms close to its body.

Disguised for hunting

The cuttlefish tightens bands of muscles under its skin. The muscles squeeze its body into different shapes so it looks like part of the sea floor. It remains still until a fish or crab comes close. Then it grabs its victim. A cuttlefish disguises itself in the same way when it is hiding from a predator, such as a seal or shark.

Cuttlefish can also quickly change the colors and patterns on their skin. They do this by sending nerve signals to cells in their skin that contain color.

WOW

A baby cuttlefish hatches from an egg. Scientists believe that the animal is born with fully formed eyes. That means that a cuttlefish can see while still inside the egg.

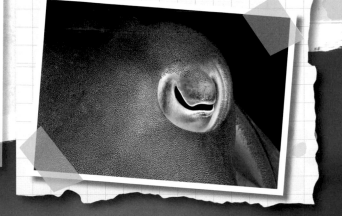

The arms of a cuttlefish hang down in front of it when the creature swims.

Birds of Paradise

Male birds of paradise use dazzling courtship displays to attract females. They fan out their colorful feathers into different shapes. Often, they do not look like birds at all.

This greater bird of paradise is fanning its tail. The bird looks bigger and brighter and more attractive to mates.

In the forest

Most birds use courtship to attract mates in the breeding season. Many male birds whistle songs to draw attention to themselves. Others grow brighter feathers to attract females. Birds of paradise are colorful birds that live on the **tropical** island of New Guinea and in parts of Australia. They live in forests and eat insects and ripe fruits. Male birds of paradise fluff out their feathers during their dramatic courtship displays. They also make clicking noises by moving their wings very fast.

A shape-shifting blue and black male bird of paradise displays its feathers to a female bird.

Most birds of paradise have dark feathers over most of the body. There are a few brighter feathers on the neck, sides, wings, and tail. During courtship, male Victoria riflebirds fan out their wings and dark breast feathers. They change their body into an oval shape.

Birds of paradise called parotias perform a different kind of shape-shift. Male parotias change their feathers into the shape of a skirt. They perform a "ballerina dance" to attract females that might be watching from a higher branch.

WOW

In New Guinea, some people use the colorful feathers of birds of paradise for their own displays. People decorate ceremonial headdresses with the feathers. Some birds of paradise are now protected to keep their feathers from being taken.

Color Change

Many animals change color. Some can change color in a flash. Others change color more slowly. Most animals that change color do so to help them blend in with their surroundings. Others change to attract a mate or to communicate with each other.

Reasons to change

Chameleons, cuttlefish, and jellyfish can change color quickly so that they match their surroundings. Sluglike sea creatures called nudibranchs change color when danger threatens. They do this to warn predators that they taste bad.

Other animals change color more slowly. Some birds **molt** their old feathers and grow bright new ones at the start of the breeding season. They do this to attract mates. For other animals, the changing seasons produce big changes in their habitat. When snow covers the land in fall and winter, Arctic foxes and hares, stoats, and birds called ptarmigans lose their brown fur and feathers and turn white to match their surroundings.

Some animals change color if they are unhealthy. A healthy flamingo is bright pink because of chemicals in the shrimp and algae it eats. If the flamingo's food lacks these chemicals, the flamingo will turn pale pink or white.

An Arctic fox becomes white in fall to match the snow.

18

ARCTIC FOXES CASE STUDY:
PAGE 22

When threatened, chameleons can change color in a few minutes.

CHAMELEONS CASE STUDY:
PAGE 20

The bright color of these flamingos shows that they are eating a healthy diet.

Chameleons

The most amazing thing about chameleons is their incredible color-changing ability. These creatures change color to attract a mate and to hide from predators.

This chameleon has caught a fly on the end of its tongue.

Life in the trees

Chameleons are **reptiles** that live in warm regions of the world. Their strong toes and sharp claws help them grip narrow branches as they climb around in trees. When a chameleon spots an insect to eat, it shoots out its long, sticky tongue. The tongue quickly snaps back into the chameleon's mouth, taking the prey with it.

The skin of chameleons is full of special cells called **chromatophores**. These can turn the animal's skin red, yellow, green, blue, purple, and pink.

This brightly colored male chameleon is showing off its colors to a female.

If a chameleon's mood changes, the chromatophores change color. A chameleon becomes darker if it feels threatened. A male may turn bright pink or turquoise to attract a female. A chameleon will turn green to blend in with its forest habitat to hide from predators.

Chameleons are cold-blooded animals. Their body temperature depends on the temperature of their surroundings. Their skin is dark early in the day. Dark colors **absorb** heat better than light colors. This helps the chameleons warm up.

COPYCAT

Scientists at the Massachusetts Institute of Technology designed screens with electronic inks that work in a similar way to the chromatophores in a chameleon's skin.

21

Arctic Foxes

The Arctic is the most northern part of Earth. In winter the land is covered with ice and snow, and the ocean freezes over. The temperature may drop to –50°F (–46°C). The Arctic fox is one of the few animals that can survive the bitter cold.

This Arctic fox is hunting for prey in summer.

Surviving the cold

The Arctic fox is a tough predator. It has a layer of fat around its body. The fat keeps its heart and other **internal** organs warm even in the middle of winter. The fox's body is covered with thick fur. So is its tail. Even its paws are furry.

The Arctic is not always frozen. In spring the weather is warmer. The brown and gray rocks beneath the snow appear as the snow melts. This is when Arctic foxes hunt for food and raise cubs. The foxes have brown and gray fur, so they are a similar color to their surroundings.

In fall, snow covers the ground. The Arctic foxes molt their brown and gray fur and grow brilliant white fur. It is hard to see a white fox walking on white snow and ice. This makes it harder for birds, hares, lemmings, and other prey to see them. The foxes can catch their prey more easily.

A fox uses its keen sense of hearing to find prey under the snow. When it hears a faint movement, the fox strikes through the snow to catch its food.

COPYCAT

Long ago people hunted Arctic foxes. They killed thousands of them for their fur. The fur was made into coats to keep people warm. Not as many people wear real fur coats now, which is one reason why the number of Arctic foxes has increased.

In winter, the Arctic fox's white coat blends in with the snow.

Camouflage

Some animals have colors, patterns, or shapes that help them blend in with their surroundings. This is called camouflage. It helps prey animals hide from predators. It helps predators hunt for prey without being seen.

Colors, patterns, and shapes

Many animals have colors and patterns that are the same as their background. Polar bears are white to blend in with snow and ice. Desert animals such as camels are often light brown to make it hard to see them in the desert sand.

Other animals have patterns that break up their body shape. This makes it more difficult to see them. The spotted coat of a leopard blends in with its grassland habitat. The stripes of a tiger's fur make the big cat harder to see in forests.

Shape is another kind of camouflage. Some animals hide from predators by looking like a different object. Stick insects look just like sticks, while planthoppers are shaped like leaves.

Some animals disguise themselves by copying the patterns and colors of another creature that is dangerous. This is called mimicry. A harmless animal is more likely to survive if predators think it is dangerous.

A mimic octopus has made itself look like a starfish to avoid being eaten.

MIMIC OCTOPUSES CASE STUDY: PAGE 28

This stick insect looks just like a twig. A hunting bird might not notice it.

This tiger is hard to see among the grasses and shadows.

TIGERS CASE STUDY: PAGE 26

Tigers

Tigers are the biggest members of the cat family. They are fearsome predators. A tiger's fur is orange with black stripes. The stripes on a tiger's fur help it hide from its prey when it is hunting. No two tigers have exactly the same pattern of stripes.

Ambush predators

Tigers are ambush predators. This means they pounce on their prey without warning. Most tigers live in forests, but some live in grasslands. The striped fur of the tiger provides excellent camouflage in these **habitats**.

Tigers that live in snowy Siberia have paler colors than tigers that live in hot, sunny forests.

A hungry tiger listens for the sound of a deer, pig, or cow moving. The tiger moves slowly and quietly to get closer to its prey. When it is close enough it leaps onto the victim and kills it. Tigers are so powerful that they can kill animals larger than themselves.

Tigers in cold lands

Most tigers live in warm parts of the world such as India, Thailand, Malaysia, and Indonesia. Snow is rare in those places. Some tigers live in colder places, though. Amur tigers live in eastern Siberia, where snow covers the ground in winter. These tigers have slightly paler fur. However, their orange and black fur does not completely camouflage them when they are in open areas covered by snow.

COPYCAT

Soldiers fighting in forests wear green or brown camouflage clothing. This keeps them hidden as they move between the trees. Soldiers sometimes wear camouflage nets.

They even put camouflage colors on their helmets and guns.

This tiger's stripes help it blend in with its forest surroundings.

Mimic Octopuses

The mimic octopus swims in shallow ocean waters around Southeast Asia. For much of the time this octopus remains hidden and camouflaged among rocks on the seafloor.

Like other octopuses, this creature is a predator. It hunts fish and crabs. When it is hungry, a mimic octopus leaves its hiding place on the seafloor. It swoops through the water and grasps its prey with its tentacles. Then the octopus draws the victim into its mouth.

A mimic octopus rests on the seafloor. This is how it looks when it is not copying another creature.

Color changers

Most octopuses can change their skin color to match their surroundings. A mimic octopus can disguise itself even better than other octopuses. It changes color and twists and folds its body into shapes that look like other sea creatures.

Different disguises

The mimic octopus can disguise itself as a dangerous animal such as a lionfish, a flounder fish, or a sea snake. If a predator thinks the octopus is more dangerous than it really is, the hunting animal will leave it alone.

A mimic octopus can also change to look like a starfish. This is not a dangerous animal, but it is tough to eat. A hungry predator might decide not to eat it.

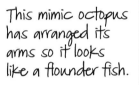

This mimic octopus has arranged its arms so it looks like a flounder fish.

WOW

Octopuses have another way to defend themselves from predators. When they feel threatened, these creatures squirt a jet of blue-black ink from a sac inside their body. The octopus then makes its escape behind a cloud of ink that spreads through the water.

Glossary

absorb to soak up

algae plantlike life forms

amphibians cold-blooded animals such as frogs and salamanders that spend part of their life in water and part of their life on land

chromatophores cells containing chemicals called pigments. These allow an animal to change color

courtship the way in which animals attract other animals to mate and produce offspring

flexible bendable

gills body parts that allow fish and young frogs to breathe in water

habitats the natural homes of animals or plants

internal on the inside of the body

larva the young form of an animal such as an insect, jellyfish, or amphibian

life cycle the stages through which a living thing passes from the start of its life until its death

mollusks soft-bodied animals such as cuttlefish and octopuses

molt when one set of skin, fur, or feathers is replaced by a new set

polyp a stage in the life cycle of a jellyfish between the planula and the adult form

predators animals that hunt and eat other animals

prey an animal that is hunted and eaten by other animals

pupa the stage in the life cycle of most insects when the larva changes into the adult form

reptiles cold-blooded animals with scaly skin, such as lizards or snakes

tentacles long, flexible arms of an animal such as an octopus

toxic containing poisonous substances

tropical warm regions to the north and south of the Equator

Read More

Kalman, Bobbie. *Animal Life Cycles: Growing and Changing*. Nature's Changes. New York: Crabtree, 2006.

Royston, Angela. *Animals that Hide*. Adapted to Survive. Oxford, England: Raintree, 2014.

Wood, Alix. *Amazing Animal Life Cycles*. Wow! Wildlife. London, England: Windmill Books, 2012.

Yaw, Valerie. *Color-Changing Animals*. Animals with Super Powers. New York: Bearport Publishing, 2011.

Internet Sites

FactHound offers a safe, fun way to find Internet sites related to this book. All of the sites on FactHound have been researched by our staff.

Here's all you do:

Visit www.facthound.com

Type in this code: 9781491469835

Super-cool stuff!

Check out projects, games and lots more at
www.capstonekids.com

Index